It's Hailing!

by Nadia Higgins

illustrated by Damian Ward

Content Consultant: Steven A. Ackerman
Professor of Atmospheric Science
University of Wisconsin-Madison

Weather Watchers

Riverhead Free Library
330 Court Street
Riverhead, NY 11901
(631) 727-3228

magic wagon

visit us at www.abdopublishing.com

Published by Magic Wagon, a division of the ABDO Group, 8000 West 78th Street, Edina, Minnesota 55439. Copyright © 2010 by Abdo Consulting Group, Inc. International copyrights reserved in all countries. All rights reserved. No part of this book may be reproduced in any form without written permission from the publisher.

Looking Glass Library™ is a trademark and logo of Magic Wagon.

Printed in the United States of America, North Mankato, Minnesota.
092009
012010

 PRINTED ON RECYCLED PAPER

Text by Nadia Higgins
Illustrations by Damian Ward
Edited by Mari Kesselring
Interior layout and design by Nicole Brecke
Cover design by Nicole Brecke

Library of Congress Cataloging-in-Publication Data
Higgins, Nadia.
   It's hailing! / by Nadia Higgins ; illustrated by Damian Ward ; content consultant, Steven A. Ackerman.
       p. cm. — (Weather watchers)
   Includes index.
   ISBN 978-1-60270-732-0
   1. Hail—Juvenile literature. I. Ward, Damian, 1977- ill. II. Title.
   QC929.H15H54 2010
   551.57'87—dc22
                                                2009029377

Table of Contents

It's Hailing!

It is a warm spring day. A dark cloud covers the sky. It looks like rain. Wait a minute.

Clink. Clink. Clink. Plunk! Balls of ice are bouncing on the sidewalk!

5

It's hailing! Those balls of ice are called hailstones. They fall down most often in spring and summer.

Most hailstorms only last about 15 minutes.

7

Up in the Sky

Where does hail come from? Hail forms way up in the sky. It is very cold up there, even in summer.

Before it hails, a few things happen. First, warm, wet air rises from Earth. Cold air sinks. A tall thundercloud forms. Then, inside the cloud, strong winds blow.

9

A hailstone
begins as a tiny
drop of frozen water
inside the thundercloud.
Wind carries the drop up
and down inside the
cloud.

The hailstone grows in the thundercloud. At the bottom of the cloud, warmer drops of water spread over the hailstone. The water freezes clear like an ice cube.

Winds carry the hailstone up where the cloud is colder. There, the water droplets hit the hailstone and freeze very quickly. This traps air bubbles, making a new layer that looks white like snow.

Over and over, a hailstone whirls inside the cloud. It picks up layer after layer of ice. These layers can be seen when a hailstone is cut in half.

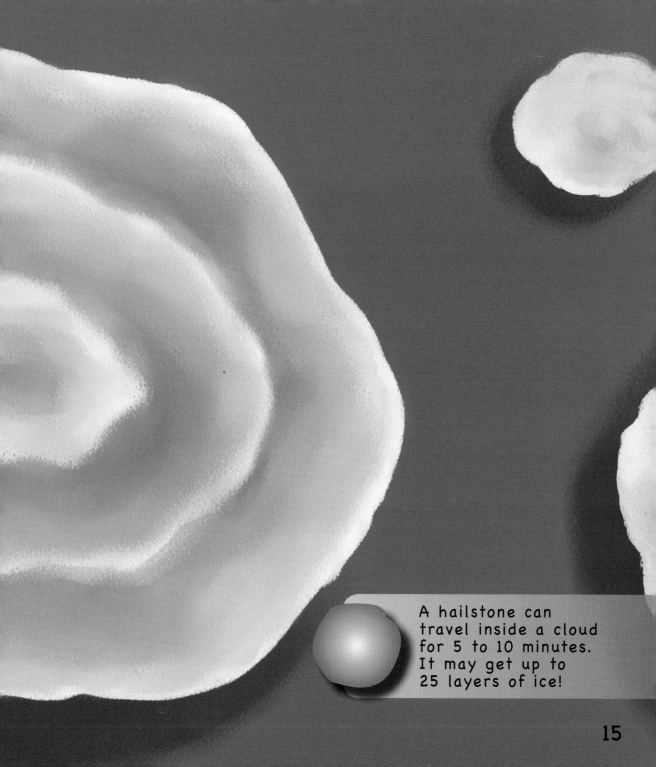

A hailstone can travel inside a cloud for 5 to 10 minutes. It may get up to 25 layers of ice!

Heavy Hailstones

Soon, the hailstone in the cloud gets too heavy. The winds can no longer carry it. It falls very quickly. It does not have time to melt.

Some hailstones fall
as fast as a car drives
on the highway.

17

Most hailstones are about the size of peas. But they can be as big as golf balls. In 2003, a huge hailstone fell in Aurora, Nebraska. It was the size of a small melon!

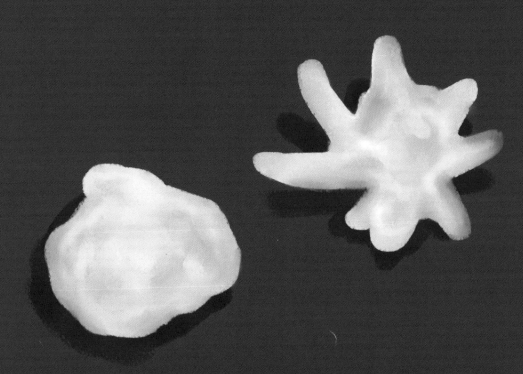

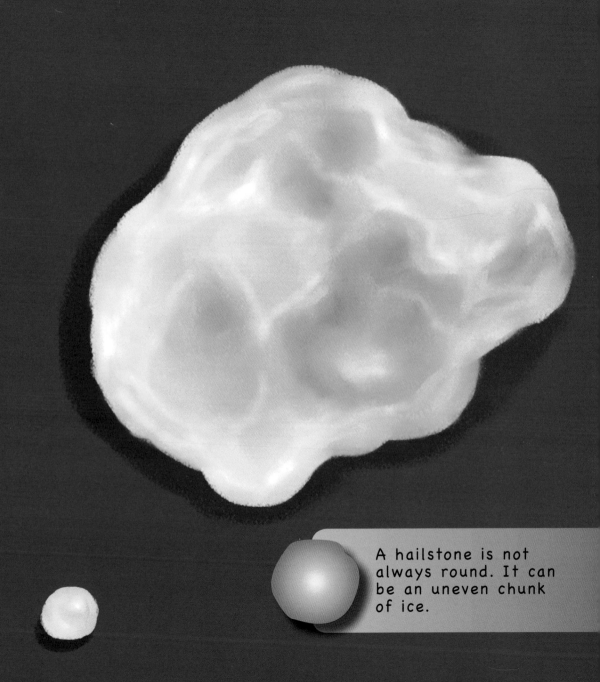

A hailstone is not always round. It can be an uneven chunk of ice.

Hailstones can cause a lot of damage. They dent cars. They break glass. And, they destroy roofs.

20

Pilots watch out for hail. It can damage an airplane's engine.

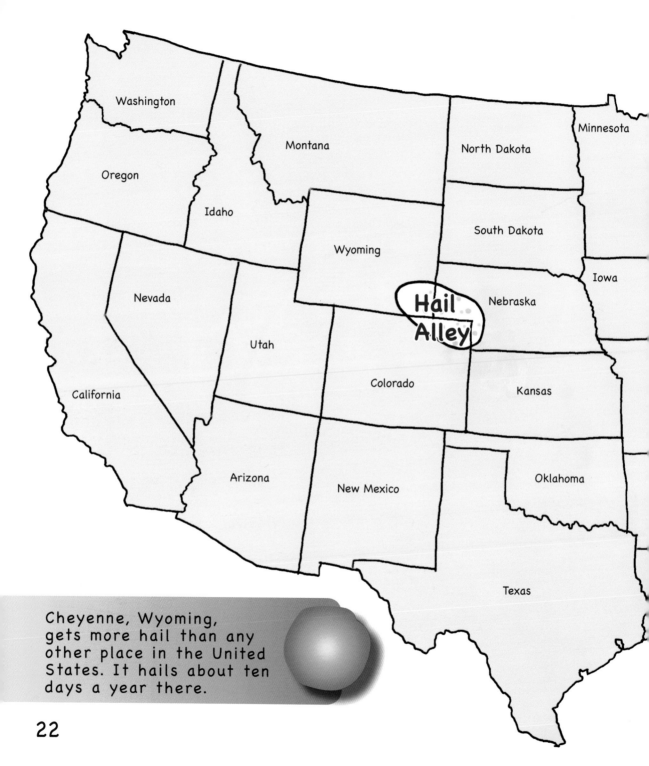

Washington

Oregon

Montana

Idaho

North Dakota

Minnesota

South Dakota

Wyoming

Hail Alley

Nebraska

Iowa

Nevada

Utah

Colorado

Kansas

California

Arizona

New Mexico

Oklahoma

Texas

Cheyenne, Wyoming, gets more hail than any other place in the United States. It hails about ten days a year there.

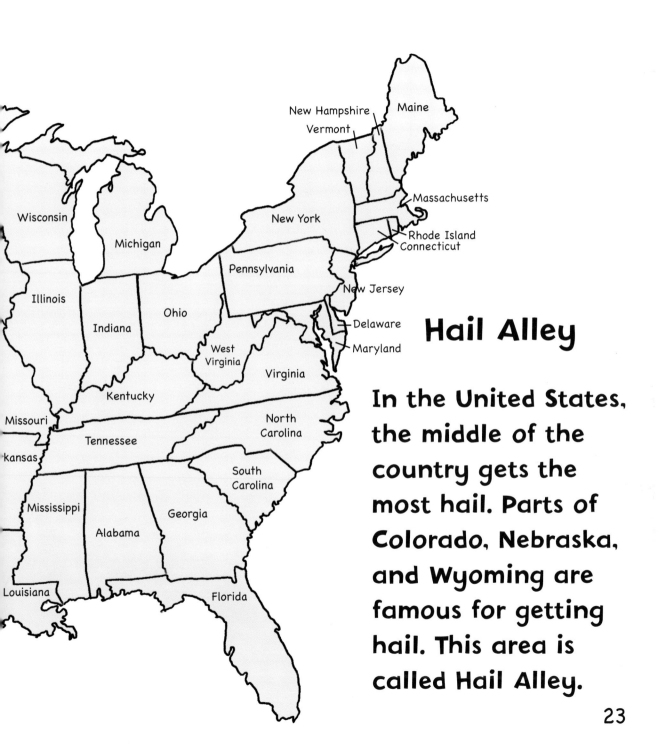

Hail Alley

In the United States, the middle of the country gets the most hail. Parts of Colorado, Nebraska, and Wyoming are famous for getting hail. This area is called Hail Alley.

23

Farmers in Hail Alley call hail the "white plague." A hailstorm can flatten a field of corn or wheat in minutes.

In Hail Alley, the "white plague" kills about one of every ten crops each year.

Is Hail on the Way?

Will it hail tomorrow? Turn on the television or radio. Listen to the weather report.

Scientists use a tool called Doppler radar. Doppler radar sends out waves of energy. When the waves hit hail, they bounce back. Scientists study the waves. They can tell where hail is and where it is going.

LIVE

AFTERNOON HAIL EXPECTED

27

If a hailstorm is coming, go inside and stay away from windows. Then, listen to the pounding ice. Enjoy some of Earth's strangest weather.

How Hail Forms

1. Hailstones begin as tiny drops of frozen water inside a thundercloud.

2. Wind carries the hailstones up and down inside the cloud. The hailstones bump into water that freezes in layers.

3. As the hailstones bump around in the cloud, they add even more layers. They get bigger.

4. The hailstones get too heavy for the wind to blow them. They fall to Earth very quickly.

Hail Facts

He Hailed from Italy
Alessandro Volta was an Italian scientist who lived in the 1700s. He was one of the first people to study hail. He cut hailstones in half and observed the layers of ice.

Deadliest Hailstorm
The worst hailstorm ever fell in Moradabad, India, in 1888. It killed more than 230 people.

Most Hail on Earth
Parts of Kenya, Africa, may get more hail than any other place on Earth. The Kericho and Nandi Hills have been known to get more than 100 days of hail per year.

Glossary

Doppler radar — a tool that scientists use to find tornadoes and track storms.

layer — a coating of something.

plague — a bad disease that spreads easily and can kill many people.

thundercloud — a huge, dark cloud that can cause hail, thunderstorms, and tornadoes.

On the Web

To learn more about hail, visit ABDO Group online at **www.abdopublishing.com**. Web sites about hail are featured on our Book Links page. These links are routinely monitored and updated to provide the most current information available.

Index